The FACT ATTACK series

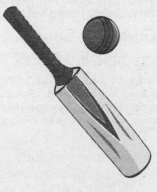

IAN LOCKE

MACMILLAN CHILDREN'S BOOKS

First published 1999 by Macmillan Children's Books

This edition published 2012 by Macmillan Children's Books
a division of Macmillan Publishers Limited
20 New Wharf Road, London N1 9RR
Basingstoke and Oxford
Associated companies throughout the world
www.panmacmillan.com

ISBN 978-1-4472-2441-9

1 3 5 7 9 8 6 4 2

A CIP catalogue record for this book is available from
the British Library.

Printed and bound by CPI Group (UK) Ltd, Croydon CR0 4YY

DID YOU KNOW THAT . . .

 W. G. Grace played his first county match in 1864, aged 16.

 A record 1,808 runs were scored in the county match between Essex and Sussex at Hove on 3 September 1993. Seven centuries were scored in the match.

 Bowler Alex Tudor of Surrey had a world record 38 runs scored off one over in a first-class match against Lancashire in June 1998. Andy Flintoff scored 34, and there were two no-balls which cost two runs each.

Emma Noble, the model once married to the son of the former British Prime Minister John Major, played cricket for the Bunbury ladies' team at Uxbridge in September 1998. She was not qualified – she knew nothing about cricket.

In 1744 a game of cricket was played on the Artillery ground near Moorgate, London, between an All-England side and Kent. It was called 'the greatest cricket match ever known'. The crowd included the Prince of Wales and the Duke of Cumberland. Kent won on the last ball after a catch was dropped. At that time there were only four balls to an over, and they were all underarm!

Ben Hollioake, 19, was called up to play for England in August 1997. The last time someone so young had been selected for England was in 1949, when Brian Close was selected.

In a Test between England and India at Lord's cricket ground which ended on 31 July 1990, 1,603 runs were scored in 1,603 minutes!

 In 1997 Surrey county cricket club decided to change its name to the Surrey Lions.

 Cricket was first mentioned in 1598, in the borough records of Guildford, England. The game was known as 'creckett'.

 The first overseas cricket match was played in 1676, in Aleppo, Syria, when English merchants played a game.

The first spin bowler in cricket history is considered to be a Mr Lamborn, 'the Little Farmer'.

 The first cricket score cards were published in 1776 by the Kent company of T. Pratt.

 A Chinaman is the name given to a ball that breaks in a way opposite to that expected by the batsman.

 During a cricket match at Home Rule in New South Wales, Australia, a fielder came across a gold nugget worth £8. As a result the cricket pitch was closed and mining renewed.

 The sports book which has sold the most in Britain was by umpire Dickie Bird – over 350,000 copies have been sold.

Ian and Greg Chappell of Australia became the first players on the same side in a Test to both score hundreds in each innings. Ian scored 145 and 121, his younger brother 247 not out and 133 against New Zealand in 1974.

 Dr M. E. Pavri, captain of the Parsee team, was pretty sure of himself. In 1889 he played on his own against a team at Metherau near Bombay, India. He scored 52 not out, and then bowled out his opponents for 38!

 In a match against Derbyshire in 1947, Peter Smith of Essex scored 163 – a record for a man at No. 11.

 The largest-selling cricket magazine in the world is *The Cricketer*. It was first published in Britain in 1921.

Denis Compton, the great English sportsman, scored a record 18 centuries in the 1947 season, beating Jack Hobbs's 1925 record of 16. He also scored a record 3,816 runs altogether, beating a record which had stood since 1906.

 In 1884, all eleven players in the England Test side playing against Australia at the Oval had a bowl. Australia scored 551 runs.

 During a match in Victoria state, at Bunbury, Western Australia, the ball was hit into a tree on the edge of the ground. It became stuck. Because the batsmen were running, it could not officially be called 'lost'. Eventually, a marksman shot down the ball with a gun. The two batsmen had, by then, run 286!

It was a long wait. Les Jackson was called up to play for England again in 1961. He'd last played for England in 1949!

 At the end of July 1998 there was a cricket match at Wembley Stadium in London. It was a unique match, between the blind England team and a W. G. Grace XI of sighted cricketers. It was a warm-up for the England team before playing in the blind players' World Cup. The cricketers used a size three football for a ball.

 During a match in July 1974, lightning struck the field, leaving a circle of burned turf on the pitch. Two fielders were blown over by the shock. The match was abandoned.

Sir Arthur Conan Doyle, the author of the Sherlock Holmes stories, said in 1921 that the name Sherlock came from the name of a Middlesex bowler. This is unlikely, but the name could have come from parts of two other cricketers' names – Shacklock and Sherwin.

 Colin Croft, the West Indies bowler, managed to make the slowest score against Australia at Brisbane in 1979. He scored only two runs in 80 minutes.

 In 1992 copies of the first three years of *Wisden* sold for £6,800 in London.

 In 1899, Arthur Edward Jeune Collins, aged 14, became a schoolboy wonder, scoring 628 not out for his house at Clifton College.

The England side beat the B's at Lord's in 1810. The B's were all out for six! They had an excuse – they only had ten men.

 King Edward IV banned cricket in England in 1479, introducing a fine and up to two years in jail for anyone caught playing the game, then known as 'hands in and hands out'.

 A copy of *Rules and Instructions for Playing at the Game of Cricket* by T. Boxall was sold for £5,500 in 1997.

 It took until 1997 for England to win their first one-day international against New Zealand.

The first Lord of cricket was English batsman Colin Cowdrey, who was given a seat in the House of Lords in June 1997.

 The first international cricket match was between Canada and the United States in New York in 1844. Canada won by 23 runs.

 The Eton–Harrow cricket match was abandoned in 1997 because of the weather. It was the first time this had happened since 1805!

 Wilson Harvey, playing for Rochdale at Walsden, Lancs, managed to hit a six through the bowler's bedroom window!

 The England side managed their first Test victory in eight years when they beat Australia at Adelaide on 30 January 1995.

In only his 18th Test match Garfield Sobers scored the then record of 305 not out against Pakistan at Kingston, Jamaica. The record was beaten by Brian Lara, with 375 at St John's, Antigua, against England. Sobers was the first to walk out to congratulate him.

 In July 1998 an archaeologist digging at Chelsea, London, came across what appeared to be a cricket bat – dating from 3540–3360 BC. It was made of oak and 75 cm long!

 In 1997, before a match played by the MCC at the private cricket ground of Talbot Radcliffe at Boderdern, Anglesey, Wales, the local groundsman (a gamekeeper by trade) had a bizarre job – he had to round up eleven ducks which were on the pitch.

Mal Loye of Northants was probably the most disappointed batsman in England in 1998. He was turned down for the England team – even though he had a batting average of 93!

 Some houses come with their own cricket pitch. Wreyland Manor near Bovey Tracey, Devon, includes the village cricket pitch in its grounds.

 The first recorded cricket match took place at Coxheath, Kent, in 1646.

 In England's record 903 for 7 declared against Australia at the Oval in 1938, Eddie Paynter managed to score 0. He had had his pads on for one and a half days before he went in.

Lisa Nye, England women's wicket-keeper, set a world record of eight dismissals in an innings, against New Zealand at Plymouth, in 1992.

 The first cricket match at Lord's was Middlesex versus Essex on 31 May 1787.

 Geoff Boycott, Derek Pringle and Chris Tavare were among the first cricketers to wear contact lenses.

 W. G. Grace scored the first and tenth of the first ten centuries scored by an English batsman.

In his last Test innings, at the Oval in August 1948, the great Australian Don Bradman received a standing ovation. He only had four runs to score to give him an almost unbeatable Test average of 100. He was bowled for 0 on the second ball.

 The famous poet Lord Byron played cricket for Harrow school in 1805 in the first recorded match against Eton school.

 In 1997 England junior cricket star Ryan Driver, aged 17, was in demand. One day he had to get up at four in the morning to fly from a two-day match for the Minor Counties at Bristol to an England schools fixture against Scottish schools in Edinburgh!

Village cricketer Rob Kelly, 24, playing for Buckland St Mary, Somerset, hit 6 sixes off an over and then hit sixes off the first five balls of the next over from another bowler in a match against the Taunton Casuals on 17 June 1993. In their innings the Casuals were all out for 24!

 In a special horse and buggy trotting race at the Globe Derby Raceway, Adelaide, Australia, Ian Botham of England, on Oh So Sensitive, beat Australian fast bowler Dennis Lillee on Bean Lincoln.

 Peter Petherick of New Zealand took a hat-trick on his debut against Pakistan in 1976–7.

 South Africa have been bowled out for less than 40 in at least four Test matches.

David Gower, the leading England batsman of the 1980s, loved having fun. In 1988 he had a bit of a problem. For a lark, after he had been out playing for England against Queensland, Australia, he went up in an ancient Tiger Moth plane. With him was fellow cricketer John Morris who had just scored a century for England. They buzzed over the ground where Lamb and Smith were still batting for England. The two surprised batsmen raised their bats and pretended to shoot down the plane! The two were recognized. It cost them a £1,000 fine – all for a £27 ride!

 Ian Botham was back in the England team in 1991 for the series against the West Indies. In the final Test at the Oval, London, he hit the winning boundary. It was the first time in 17 years that England hadn't lost to the West Indies. The match was also the last appearance of the legendary Viv Richards – he was retiring from West Indies Tests. His team had never lost a series while he was their captain.

When he appeared in his last Test match for England in 1930, against the West Indies, at Kingston, Jamaica, Wilf Rhodes of Yorkshire was 52 years and 165 days old. He was the oldest Test cricketer ever. He took 4,187 wickets in his career.

 Only one score over 850 was made in first-class cricket in the 19th century – in a match between Yorkshire and Warwickshire at Birmingham. The score was 887.

 After David and Rosa Lacey said they lived in fear of being hit by cricket balls, the players of the Jordans cricket team in Buckinghamshire introduced a new rule. Anyone who hit a six on either side of the village green was given out!

India beat England in all the Tests in 1993 – the first time since the two countries began playing each other in 1933.

 The first twins to score a century for different sides in the same match were Mark and Steve Waugh of Australia. Mark scored for Essex and his brother scored for the Australian tourists, in 1989.

 The first ever county cricket match was between Kent and London in 1709.

 In the Northampton against Somerset match in 1914, the first pair to bat for Northants were the Denton twins. Somerset had the Rippon twins in their team.

 The first cricketer to be knighted was Frederick Toone.

Clem Hill of Australia was the first Test player out for 99, against England in 1902. In his next two innings he scored 98 and 97!

Tom Moody scored a century in a world record 26 minutes in 1990 in the county championships, playing for Warwickshire against Glamorgan.

By 23 May 1994 Brian Lara, the West Indies batsman, had scored 884 runs in his last five first-class innings, with an amazing average of 221. He scored his fifth successive hundred at Taunton in only 72 deliveries.

There have only been two Test ties in history. The first took place in the first Test at Brisbane, Australia, in 1960, between the Australians and New Zealand. On the last ball Joe Solomon of the West Indies ran Meckiff out. The second took place in 1986 between Australia and India.

The man who bought Lord's cricket ground in 1825 for £5,000, William Ward, was MP for the City of London. He sold the ground for £18,000 in 1866.

 Micky Stewart, the England Test player and father of Alec, also played football for Charlton Athletic FC.

 In 1893 W. G. Grace managed to score 93 – which meant he had then achieved every score between 0 and 100.

 All seven Forster brothers played for Worcestershire. It is said their father, a vicar, tested their fielding and catching by using the family crockery.

The cricketer's bible, *Wisden's Almanac*, was first published by John Wisden and Co. in 1864. It cost one shilling (5p). A paperback, it had 116 pages. The price reached 25p in 1921 and 75p in 1956. In 1920 it had 327 pages and in 1921 727 pages.

 A record 394,000 crowd watched the Test between India and England at Eden Gardens, Calcutta, in January 1982.

 On 7 June 1993 Graham Gooch became the first English Test cricketer (and only the fifth batsman ever, at that point in time) to be dismissed for handling the ball. He was playing for England against Pakistan at Old Trafford.

 When aged 74 Lionel Deamer took a hat-trick for Lloyds Bank vs. Eastwood cricket club, on 6 July 1979.

During the 1990 season in England 428 centuries were scored.

 On a scorching day in Sydney in 1979, England were down to only one bowler, Ian Botham, after Bob Willis had gone off dehydrated. Botham went on to bowl 18 overs!

 A Surrey and All-England cricketer in the 19th century had the name Julius Caesar!

In the England vs. South Africa Test series of 1913–14, Sydney Barnes, the English bowler, refused to play in the fifth Test after a dispute. In the first four Tests he had taken a record 49 wickets!

 Woman cricketer Mabel Bryant scored 224 runs in 135 minutes for the Visitors vs. the Residents at Eastbourne, Sussex, in 1901!

 Hedley Verity, a slow left-arm bowler for Yorkshire and England, took 10 wickets for 10 runs in a Yorkshire vs. Nottinghamshire match at Leeds in 1932.

 Doug Walters of Australia, playing the West Indies in the fifth Test at Sydney on 18 February 1969, became the first batsman to score a century and a double century in the same Test match.

The English film actor C. Aubrey Smith, nicknamed 'Round the Corner' Smith for his bowling style, looked after the British cricket team in Hollywood from the 1920s. His Hollywood home had a weathervane of three stumps and a cricket bat and ball.

 The first non-white cricketer to play for South Africa in Tests was Omar Henry, aged 41, in 1992.

 In 1993, on South Africa's official peace day, 2 September, the South African cricket team stood for a minute's silence on the ground at Colombo, Sri Lanka. They were in the middle of playing a one-day international match.

Ian Botham, the great England all-rounder, made front-page headlines in 1981, when he swung an almost impossible win for England against Australia at the Headingley Test. He blasted 149 not out in England's second innings. For the last three wickets England put on a massive 221. Australia still looked like winning – they only had to score 130. But they collapsed as England paceman Bob Willis took 8 wickets for 43 runs. England won this extraordinary and historic Test by 18 runs.

 Charles Kortright of Essex bowled the only six byes in history, at Wallingford. His ball went straight over the batsman and the wicketkeeper. He was one of the fastest bowlers of all time.

 William Light, who played professional cricket for Exeter and Devon, bowled with both his left and right arm.

On 13 March 1993, Indian batsman Vinod Kambli, who was only 21, became only the third player to score successive double centuries in Tests. The others were Walter Hammond (England) and Sir Don Bradman (Australia). Kambli scored 224 against England in February and then 207 not out against Zimbabwe at Delhi.

 During a match on Salisbury Plain, on the island of St Helena, the batsman made a long hit. The fielder set off after the ball. Forgetting where he was, he fell over the cliff on the edge of the pitch and died on the rocks below.

 Cricket is about records and other numbers. These include:

61,237. The record total of runs scored by Jack Hobbs of England in his first-class career.

4,204. The most wickets taken in a first-class career – by Wilfred Rhodes.

643. The number of minutes Mike Atherton

of England batted to save the second Test against South Africa in 1995 – he scored 185 runs.

501. The score which Brian Lara reached when batting for Warwickshire against Durham.

800. Muttiah Muralitharan of Sri Lanka's record for the most wickets in Test matches.

44. The number of wickets taken by Clarrie Grimmett for Australia in the Test series against South Africa in 1935–6.

20. The world record number of sixes in an innings – by Andrew Symonds of Gloucester against Glamorgan at Abergavenny in 1995. This record was matched in 2011 by Essex's Graham Napier against Surrey.

11. Jack Russell held this record number of catches in Tests, in the second Test against South Africa in 1995.

7. Dominic Cork of England took this number of wickets in the second innings of his debut Test, against the West Indies in 1995.

When a player took the wrong bus for a game at Kensington, London, and failed to show up, the umpire gave him out. A ball had not yet been bowled.

 It is not often a batsman 'carries the bat' all the way through an innings. Geoff Boycott managed it for England against Australia at Perth in 1979 – but he was not pleased – he scored 99 not out!

 Only three batsmen have ever scored over 50 hundreds – with at least one century every five and a half innings – Lindsay Hassett (Australia), Donald Bradman (Australia) and Graeme Hick (England).

On 26 February 1975, Ewan Chatfield, the New Zealand cricketer, 'died' on the pitch for three or four seconds, after being hit on the head with a ball. Given first aid, he recovered, with only a slight fracture of his skull.

 A cricket spectator at Olveston, Sussex, was twice hit by sixes during a game on 13 June 1995.

 The poet Wordsworth was responsible for bringing about the Oxford vs. Cambridge cricket matches, in 1827.

 Muttiah Muralitharan holds the record for most wickets – with 501 wickets.

Somerset CC won their first trophy for 104 years in September 1979, beating Northamptonshire in the Gillette cup final. The very next day they won the John Player League championships by beating Nottinghamshire.

 Mike Atherton has taken only one wicket in Test matches. It cost 282 runs.

 It took two and a half hours for the umpires to decide that Alvin Kallicharran of the West Indies was not run out during a Test against England in 1974.

 The Oval cricket ground was originally a vegetable garden. Surrey played their first match there in 1846.

On 1 May 1946 Frederick Stocks of Nottingham scored a century – on his first-class debut against Kent at Trent Bridge. He took a wicket with his first ball bowled in first-class cricket against Lancashire at Old Trafford on 26 June 1946.

 A game at the South Pole in 1969 had to end when the only ball was lost in the snow. The wicket was the Pole itself – a striped pole with a glass bowl on top.

 In 1979 the speed of a ball bowled by the legendary Australian fast bowler Jeff Thompson was measured at 91.86 miles per hour!

A magpie delayed the start of a match at Ryde, Isle of Wight, in the summer of 1998. It stole the keys to the motorized roller used on the pitch and the teams had to wait until a tractor arrived.

Glenn McGrath, the Australian pace bowler, has an unusual and not very nice occupation on his days off – he goes shooting pigs on his outback estate.

Australian cricketer Victor Trumper died in Sydney on 28 June 1915, aged 38. The crowd was so big for his funeral that the streets of the city were blocked. Eleven Australian cricketers carried his coffin.

In 1870 a player called Summers was killed by a cricket ball while playing at Lord's.

At Nottingham in 1877 the great W. G. Grace took 17 wickets for an average of under 5 runs!

 One of the greatest throws in cricket was accomplished by R. Percival in 1884 – he threw the ball a massive 128 metres (140 yards).

 In May 1895 W. G. Grace became the first English cricketer to score over 1,000 runs.

When playing for Kent against Middlesex at Hove, the great batsman Ranjitsinhji came in. Kent faced defeat since no one apart from Vine had scored double figures and Vine had only managed 17. The 'prince' decided to stay in – and went on to score 202!

Pat Morphy, a Kent cricketer, was able to hold six cricket balls in one hand. He is believed to have had the largest hands in the history of cricket.

 The founder of *Wisden*, John Wisden, had a unique record – he took all 11 wickets for the North, against the South at Lord's in 1850 – all clean bowled!

 In the 19th century the Oval cricket ground in London held walking races or poultry shows when cricket was not being played.

 During the Second World War, the England bowler Jim Laker was sent to Egypt. He joined the cricket club El Alamein and changed his bowling to off-spin. This change was to make him one of the most devastating bowlers in cricket history.

A bomb scare stopped play on the third day of the third Test at Lord's between England and the West Indies on 25 August 1973.

 Musical bands played at Test matches in Australia until 1931.

 Australian batsman Trumper was working in his shop in Sydney, Australia, one Saturday morning when he suddenly realized that he needed to be at the Test match! Snatching a coat and his new bat he caught a taxi to the Sydney cricket ground just in time. He went on to make 185 not out.

 W. G. Grace took his new wife on honeymoon for his tour of Australia in 1873 – the journey by ship took 49 days. Grace was keen to go, as he was being paid £1,000 (about £100,000 today) to play for England.

Early cricket bats of the 18th century were fairly large – over a metre tall.

 During the Test at Lord's between England and the West Indies in 1939, the crowd were asked to volunteer for National Service in the armed forces.

 Women are said to have invented overarm bowling in 1805, to avoid catching their fashionably wide crinoline skirts while playing cricket!

When the Australians played South Africa for the first time in the early 1900s, people reckoned they wouldn't make many runs because the South African pitches were so different from those in Australia. They had a surprise when, in his very first match, the Australian Trumper scored over 200!

When playing at the Oval, Jack Hobbs of England once gave himself out – even after the Australian umpire said he was not out.

Straight upright cricket bats, rather than curved ones, were introduced by John Small senior in 1773. They only came into regular use in the early 1800s.

In 1934 a cricket match in India was interrupted by five terrorists. Colonel Brett, who was batting, chased them off and was awarded the Empire Gallantry medal for his action.

Frederick, Prince of Wales, son of
George II, died in 1751 as a result
of being hit by a cricket ball while
playing on the lawn at Cliveden
House, Buckinghamshire.

 During World War Two, the big roller from
Lord's cricket ground was sent to the Far
East. It was used to roll out the ground for
airstrips for Allied planes!

 A Surrey cricket team played a team
from Kent in 1730. All the Surrey
players had the surname Wood!

 During February 1991 a cricket match
was played between the St Moritz and
Cresta cricket clubs on a frozen lake at
St Moritz, Switzerland. The players wore
spiked shoes and ski gloves. The St Moritz
side, which included former England
captain Chris Cowdrey, won.

In 1991 a judge decided the result of a cricket match between Delhi and Punjab, India. The argument was over a replacement umpire. Punjab was awarded the match, even though Delhi had beaten them by 9 wickets!

 A sculpted cricket bat, ball and pair of stumps were on the gravestone of the cricketer Richard Barlow, of Lancashire and England, who died on 31 July 1919. He was an umpire for 21 years. The last line reads: 'Bowled at last.'

 A 24-hour cricket match was played at Parker's Piece ground, Cambridge, in June 1973. Roger Coates scored a century in the early hours of the morning.

 William Adlam played cricket at the age of 104 at Taunton, Somerset, in 1888.

The author J. M. Barrie founded his own cricket team, the Allah Kbarres – named after the Arabic for 'heaven help us'. His team included the famous authors P. G. Wodehouse and Arthur Conan Doyle. P. G. Wodehouse once scored 60 in a match between Authors and Publishers at Lord's, including one six and ten fours. He went on to take four wickets when bowling.

Viv Richards, the great West Indies batsman, played football for his native Antigua in a world cup qualifier match.

The first googly was bowled in a match between Middlesex and Leicester at Lord's by Bernard James Tindal Bosanquet in July 1900. The Australians still call it a 'bosie' in his memory.

The first world cup cricket competition took place in 1995. The cup was a silver trophy found in a London jeweller's dating from 1882.

During practice at Oxford in 1856, the Rev. W. Fellows is said to have hit a ball from Charles Rogers 175 yards (160 metres).

Lord Home of the Hirsel is the only British prime minister to play first-class cricket.

At the Oval in 1964, Ted Dexter's bat split in two while he played.

On 13 June 1995 Australian cricketer Andrew Symonds managed to hit the same woman spectator twice in the same game with sixes.

Fifteen balls were used in the second England vs. Australia Test in 1924–5, as a result of inferior balls being supplied.

 In 1995 South Africa became only the second team in Test match history to win a three-match series after losing the opening game (against New Zealand). Over 100 years before, in 1888, W. G. Grace had led England to a similar 2–1 win over Australia.

 By pure coincidence, the result of the 'centenary' Test of 1977, celebrating 100 years of England vs. Australia, was the same as the very first Test the two sides played – Australia won by 45 runs.

In the 1930s a 20 kg (45 lb) salmon was caught in cricket nets at the Worcestershire county cricket ground, after the River Severn, which ran by the ground, burst its banks.

In the whole history of cricket, there are only seven batsmen who have been out for 99 in both innings of a Test. The only two current players to have managed this rare achievement are Michael Atherton of England and Greg Blewett of Australia.

During the Australia vs. England Test at the Oval in 1921, the Australian captain W. W. Armstrong became bored. He went to the edge of the pitch and read a newspaper.

Don Bradman of Australia was both the youngest and the oldest player to score a double century, aged almost 22 in 1930 and aged 38 in 1946.

 Columbia records signed the great Australian cricketer Don Bradman in 1930. They thought they would be recording a good dose of talk about cricket. Instead they got a medley of piano tunes played by Bradman, including 'Our Bungalow of Dreams'.

 Play at Lord's was first interrupted by a streaker in 1975.

 The Australia vs. England Test at Headingley in 1975 never finished. Play had to be abandoned after vandals dug up parts of the pitch and poured oil on it. It was a protest over the jailing of London robber George Davis.

The England vs. Australia Test match of 1888 at Lord's lasted only 7 hours and 20 minutes.

 Sir Donald Bradman made his first century aged 12 when at the Bowral High school.

 2,000 stormed the pitch in a match between New South Wales and Lord Harris's XI in 1879, after one of the English team insulted the crowd. Lord Harris was the only one to stay on the pitch, under the impression that the match would be forfeit if he left. After 90 minutes of mayhem, the game was abandoned.

 Mike Brearley, the very successful England captain of the 1970s, always hummed as he batted.

The record 'C'mon, Aussie, C'mon', made by the Australian world series cricket team, reached No. 1 in the charts in Australia.

 Test series between Australia and England are played for the Ashes. When the third Australian team to visit thrashed England at the Oval, the newspaper the *Sporting Times* wrote about the death of English cricket. The article said, 'The body will be cremated and the ashes taken to Australia.' When England defeated Australia the following year, the stumps used were burned and presented to the English captain by the Australian captain.

 From May 1995 to September 1998 Jason Barry played cricket in 52 countries, travelling 350,000 miles. The British foreign office was among his sponsors.

The first women's cricket match was held between two Surrey villages on 26 July 1945.

 You can sometimes be dropped from the side when things seem to be going well. David Gower was dropped by England for the fifth Test against the West Indies in 1988 when he'd just reached 7,000 Test runs!

 In the fourth Test at Sydney in 1883, the England and Australian captains agreed to play each innings on a separate pitch.

 In 1866 batsman G. Wells managed to be out before the ball was bowled! Playing for Sussex against Kent at Gravesend, he hit wicket as the bowler ran in and was given out!

The England wicketkeeper Godfrey Evans won £1,000 on the TV quiz show *Double Your Money* in 1964. He didn't answer questions about cricket, but about jewellery! He gave half the money to charity.

 A pig was let loose during the fourth one-day international between England and Australia at Brisbane, Australia, in January 1983. On one side of it was stamped Botham and on the other Eddie – the England players Ian Botham and Eddie Hemmings were both said to be overweight.

 Forget about winning the game – we won the Pools. In March 1961 a syndicate of 22 sportsmen and showbusiness people won £41,231 on the Pools. They included cricketers Freddie Trueman and Jim Laker – also Jimmy Hill and racing driver Jack Brabham.

George VI may be the only man to bowl out two kings – he dismissed his father George V and his brother Edward VIII in successive balls.

 After Australian batsman Victor Trumper broke a window in a factory 150 metres away from the pitch in 1902, the owners kept the broken window as a memento!

 During a match in Hull in July 1876, W. G. Grace hit a ball an almighty crack. It ended up in a passing railway truck – and was later found 37 miles away in Leeds!

 Charles Fry was an amazing British sportsman. In 1893 he equalled the world long-jump record, and in 1901 he played soccer for England and rugby for the Barbarians. He became England cricket captain in 1912, and scored the highest number of runs of any English player for six seasons!

The snooker player Eddie Charlton was a good cricketer – he was so good an all-round athlete that he carried the Olympic torch at the Melbourne Games, Australia, in 1956.

 During an Australian match in November 1969, John Iverarity was clean bowled by a ball that hit a bird just before it hit the wicket. The umpire decided it was the bird, not the ball, that bowled him and he was given 'not out'.

 Australian batsman Graeme Yallop was the first Test player to officially wear a helmet. It was in the Test against the West Indies at the Kensington Oval, Barbados, in March 1978.

England beat Australia for the first time in almost seven years on 23 August 1993 in the fifth Test at the Oval. England won by 161 runs. They had last beaten Australia in December 1986.

The world record price for a cricket bat stands at $145,000. It was paid in 2008 for the bat owned by Donald Bradman.

It was one of most spectacular matches ever. Against all odds England managed to pull off a famous victory in the third Cornhill Test against Australia in 1981. The odds (estimated by the former England player Godfrey Evans) were 500–1. To everyone's surprise, among those who bet on an England win were the Australian players Dennis Lillee and Rodney Marsh.

While putting his sweater on, A. R. Gover managed to take a catch between his legs during a match at Kingston in 1946.

 During commentary on a Middlesex vs. Sussex match, where John Warr was one of the captains, Brian Johnston managed to say, 'The latest news here is that Warr's declared'.

 Ants stop play! Flying ants stopped a cricket match between Alvechurch & Hopwood and Dominies & Guild, at Worcester in August 1998.

 One of the four stamps issued for the bicentenary of Australia in 1988 actually pictured not an Australian, but the English cricketer W. G. Grace!

One of the unexpected fans of the former English umpire Dickie Bird is the American horror writer Stephen King.

 The Oval cricket ground is owned by Prince Charles, as Duke of Cornwall. The Prince of Wales's feathers are displayed in the ground.

 Sachin Tendulkar of India has made more centuries than anyone else – 51 in all.

 The father of the famous British author H. G. Wells was a professional cricketer.

 The West Indies abandoned their England tour so they could catch the boat home before World War Two broke out in 1939.

At a July 1995 match of 'Kwik Cricket' at the Oval with children, Wajid Khan, aged 10, bowled out Prince Charles first ball.

 George Headley has the highest average of a West Indian batsman in Tests – at 60.63 runs per innings.

Jim Laker, the England bowler, took all 10 Australian wickets for 88 runs on 16 May 1956 at the Oval.

In 1993, Alan Border of Australia set a world record for runs, catches, playing in Test matches and being captain of his country. He retired in 1994 after Australia won the World Series cricket final against South Africa.

After he had scored 174 runs in the Centenary Test at Melbourne in 1977, England player Derek Randall was sent 174 pork chops by a Nottingham butcher.

 In July 1981, Gladstone Small, the Warwickshire bowler, was fined £50 for wearing an advertisement on his bottom. The manager took sticky plaster and a pair of scissors on to the pitch to cover it up.

 On one of his school reports, a master wrote that Ian Botham would be 'nothing but a waster'.

 A farmer called Lambert invented the off-break at Hambledon, Hampshire, in the 17th century.

Surrey leave the Oval for a game
at Guildford once a year. They first
started playing a match at Guildford in
1938.

 When he bowled, which wasn't
often, Geoff Boycott always kept
his cap on.

 During the 1977 England tour of Pakistan
and New Zealand, Bob Willis carried
around tapes for hypnotism. He said they
helped.

Alfred Shaw, an ex-England cricket captain who died in 1907, had a last wish – to be buried 22 yards from bowler Arthur Shrewsbury. Shrewsbury had committed suicide in 1903. The distance between the two graves turned out to be 27 yards, because Shrewsbury always took a five-yard run-up!

 The strangest Test match took place in January 1998 – the first Test between England and the West Indies at Sabina Park, Jamaica. It became the first Test match ever to be halted because of a dangerous pitch and lasted 56 minutes of playing time and only 62 deliveries. England had scored 17 for 3 when, at 11.45 a.m., the match was abandoned as a draw.

George Mann became captain of the England cricket side in 1948 – his father had also been captain.

 In 1990 David Gower was called in to play for England in a match at Barbados, West Indies, because so many of the England team were sick. He'd only been in Barbados to cover the England tour for the media!

 England cricketers Ed Giddins and Naseem Shahid set up a business to sell Christmas trees in December 1998.

The batting helmet for cricket is said to have been invented by Mrs Hendren, wife of Elias 'Patsy' Hendron. She sewed on extra peaks to his cap to help protect his face while batting.